Busy Machines
Diggers

Written by Amy Johnson   Illustrated by Kirsten Collier

Miles Kelly

Ready to build!

All day long, machines are hard at work on the building site. There are diggers and dumpers, loaders and lifters.

They SCRAPE...

Excavator

Crane

Concrete mixer

Dumper truck

and RATTLE...

and RUMBLE.

Bulldozer

Diggers at work

Most **excavators** have caterpillar tracks that keep them steady on bumpy ground.

Backhoe

A **backhoe loader** has an arm for digging at the back and a bucket for scooping at the front.

Tractor

Loader bucket

Monster miner

This is one of the world's biggest machines! It's called a **bucket wheel excavator**. It is used in mines to dig out huge amounts of soil and rock.

Conveyor belts carry the rock away

The bucket wheel is attached to a long arm

The heavy excavator sits on lots of caterpillar tracks that crawl along

keep it moving

Meet the tough transporters — machines made for lifting, moving, shifting and scooping.

Forklift

Backhoe loader

Wheel loader

Giant bulldozer

Boom lift

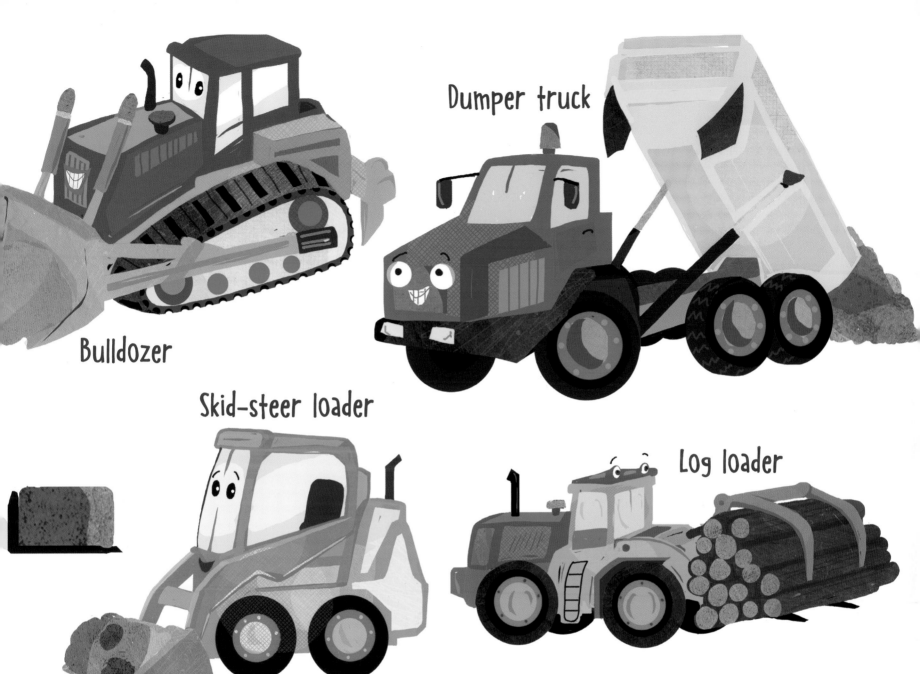

Bulldozer

Dumper truck

Skid-steer loader

Log loader

Earth scraper

Tracked loader

All about excavators

Munching up the ground, digging holes and scooping up heavy loads, **excavators** are very busy building machines.

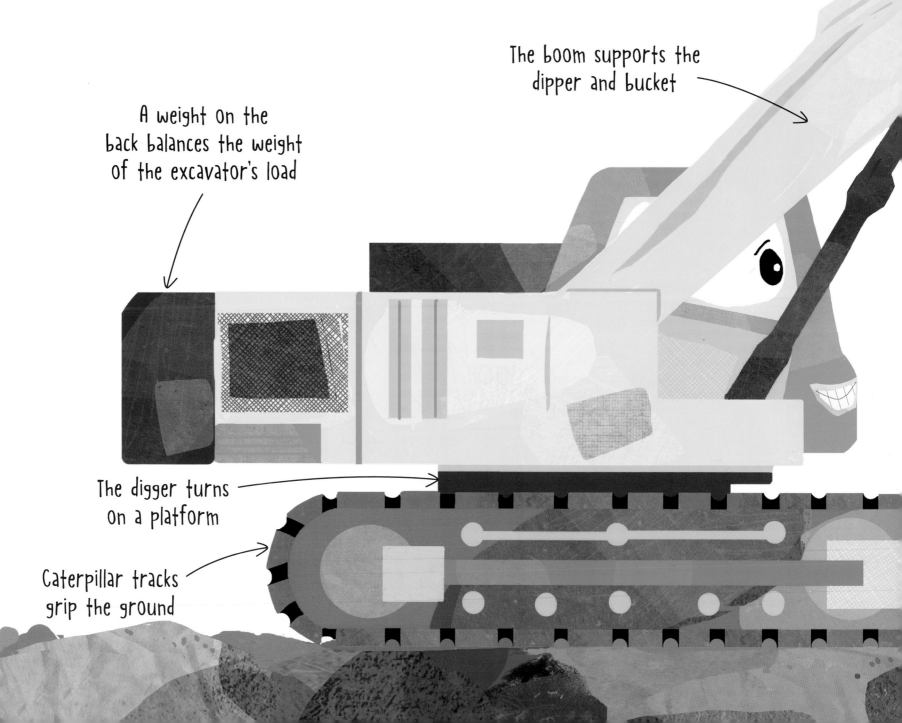

The boom supports the dipper and bucket

A weight on the back balances the weight of the excavator's load

The digger turns on a platform

Caterpillar tracks grip the ground

The dipper drags the bucket through the ground

Breaker

Grapple

The dipper can have other tools attached.

Drill

An edge of tough teeth helps the bucket bite into the ground

Busy machines!

Find your favourite building machine!

Rock busters

Deep in a massive pit, it's the job of tough machines to dig rock from the ground.

Massive **dumper trucks** carry away huge amounts of rock.

A **rock crusher** breaks up big pieces of rock and shoots out smaller bits.

Using a big metal blade, **bulldozers** push earth and rock out of the way.

Excavators scoop out rock and load it into the dumper trucks.

Wheel loaders move rocks to the dumper trucks or the crusher.

Grapples are used to pick up big rocks.

sky high

Tower cranes stay in one spot for months at a time, working high above the ground. They help build very tall buildings.

These blocks balance the weight

The operator has to climb a ladder all the way up to the cab

This tall tower is called a mast

The arm is called a jib. It moves up and down and from side to side

The main arm is called a boom

All about dumper trucks

One of the biggest building machines, dumper trucks are always on the go. They carry great piles of earth, rubble and rock.

The box tilts up to let its load slide out.

Huge tyres give plenty of grip

The canopy protects the cab and engine from falling rocks

Powerful engine

There are ladders for the driver to reach the cab

on the road

A new road is taking shape. Massive earth-movers have cleared the way — now it's time to start Building!

1 Dirt is added. Bulldozers move and shape the earth.

2 The grader uses its long blade to make a flat surface.

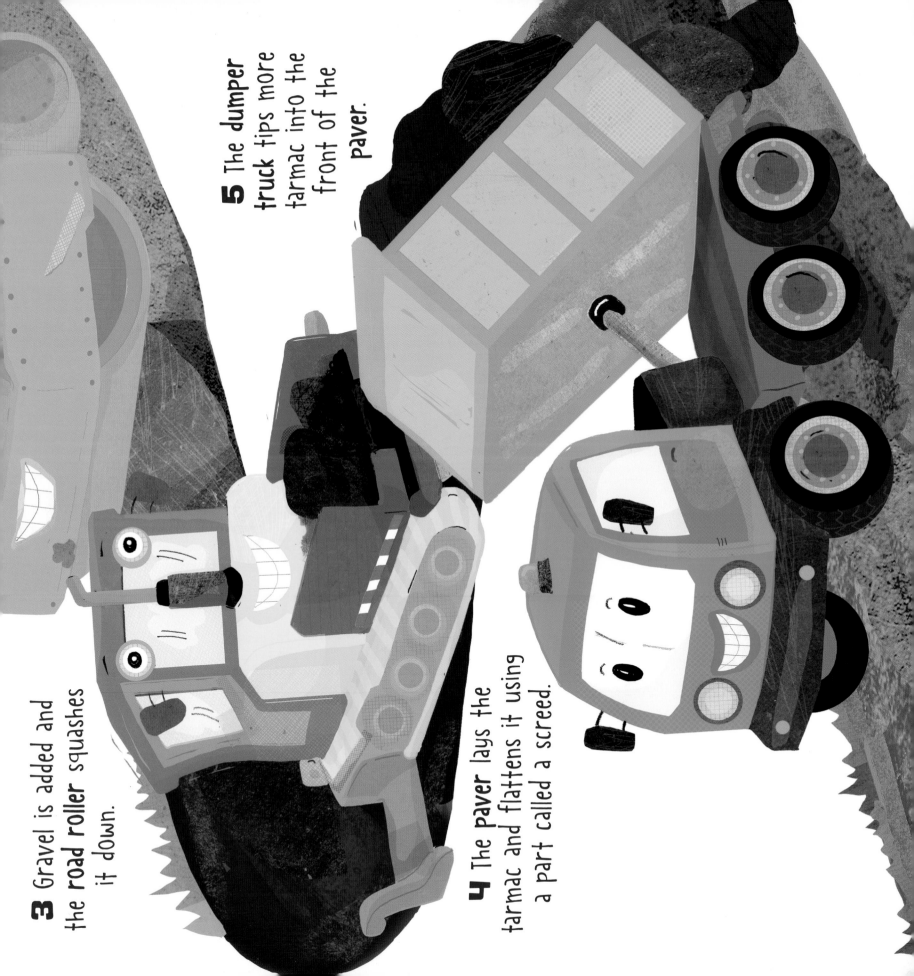

3 Gravel is added and the **road roller** squashes it down.

4 The **paver** lays the tarmac and flattens it using a part called a screed.

5 The **dumper truck** tips more tarmac into the front of the paver.

smash, crash, crumble

It takes a crew of demolition excavators to tear old buildings down! They have extra-long arms for reaching up high.

First, **skid-steer loaders** take apart the insides of a building.

Then the **excavators** get to work!

Excavators use different tools for different jobs. I'm a pulverizer. I'm great at chomping through concrete and metal!

Walking wonder

To a **walking excavator**, no terrain is too tough! It tackles water, unsteady ground and steep slopes.

On the end of the boom is a bucket or another tool for digging

The boom can also work as an extra leg, stretching across big gaps

Having four legs means I can dig in places other machines can't reach!